High-Interest/ Low-Readability
Miles Masters' Mystery Diaries

Ten Fictional High-Interest Mysteries
Written as the Diary Entries
of 12 Year Old Mystery Magnet — Miles Masters
Complete with Comprehension Activities and Audio CD

by
Jo Browning-Wroe
and
Sherrill B. Flora

illustrated by
Julie Anderson

D1709798

Publisher
Key Education Publishing Company, LLC
Minneapolis, Minnesota
www.keyeducationpublishing.com

CONGRATULATIONS ON YOUR PURCHASE OF A KEY EDUCATION PRODUCT!

The editors at Key Education are former teachers who bring experience, enthusiasm, and quality to each and every product. Thousands of teachers have looked to the staff at Key Education for new and innovative resources to make their work more enjoyable and rewarding. Key Education is committed to developing and publishing educational materials that will assist teachers in building a strong and developmentally appropriate curriculum for young children.

PLAN FOR GREAT TEACHING EXPERIENCES WHEN YOU USE
EDUCATIONAL MATERIALS FROM KEY EDUCATION PUBLISHING COMPANY, LLC

Credits
Authors: Sherrill B. Flora and
Jo Browning-Wroe
Art Director: Annette Hollister-Papp
Illustrator: Julie Anderson
Editor: George C. Flora
Production: Key Education Staff
Audio CD: The voice of Miles Masters
Jeff Standke

Key Education welcomes manuscripts and product ideas from teachers. For a copy of our submission guidelines, please send a self-addressed, stamped envelope to:
Key Education Publishing Company, LLC
Acquisitions Department
7309 West 112th Street
Bloomington, Minnesota 55438

About the Author of the Stories:

Jo Browning Wroe has taught both in the United Kingdom and in the United States. She earned her undergraduate degrees in English and Education from Cambridge University, Cambridge, England. She worked for twelve years in educational publishing before completing a Masters Degree in Creative Writing from the University of East Anglia, Norwich, England. Most of her time is now spent writing teacher resource materials and running workshops for others who love to write. Jo has been the recipient of the National Toy Libraries Award. She lives in Cambridge, England with her two daughters, Alice and Ruby, and her husband, John.

About the Author of the Activities:

Sherrill B. Flora is the Publisher of Key Education. Sherrill earned her undergraduate degrees in Special Education and Child Psychology from Augustana College and a Masters Degree in Educational Administration from Nova University. Sherrill spent ten years as a special education teacher in the inner city of Minneapolis before beginning her twenty-year career in educational publishing. Sherrill has authored over 100 teacher resource books, as well as hundreds of other educational games and classroom teaching aids. She has been the recipient of three Director's Choice Awards, three Parent's Choice Awards, and a Teacher's Choice Award. She lives in Minneapolis, Minnesota with her two daughters, Katie and Kassie, and her very supportive husband, George.

Standard Book Number: 978-1-933052-74-8
High-Interest/Low Readability:
Miles Master's Mystery Diaries
Copyright © 2007 by Key Education Publishing Company, LLC
Bloomington, Minnesota 55438

Introduction

About the Stories

All of the stories and activities found in *High Interest/Low Readability: Miles Masters' Mystery Diaries* have been specifically designed for students who are reading below grade level; for students who have reading disabilities; and for students who are reluctant or discouraged readers.

The engaging stories are written between early-first grade and late-second grade reading levels. Each story's specific reading level and word count can be found above the story title on the Table of Contents (page 4). This information will help guide the teacher in choosing stories that are appropriate for the individual needs of the students. (Reading grade levels are not printed on any of the stories or on any of the reproducible activity pages.)

Since struggling readers are often intimidated and easily overwhelmed by small print, each story was created with a large easy-to-read font. The large font, picture clues, and sentence structure will help the children feel more self-confident as they read the stories included in *Miles Masters' Mystery Diaries.*

All of the stories use high-frequency words and essential vocabulary. A list of the story's high-frequency words, as well as any special words that are necessary for each story are found on pages 61 and 62. Prior to reading each story, review the word lists and introduce and practice any unfamiliar words. Make flash cards of the new words and outline each letter with glitter glue to provide a tactile experience for the students. Draw a picture of the word on each card to help the students visualize any new vocabulary.

About the Audio CD: "Mile's Recorded Diary"

Each story comes with its own auditory diary — read by Miles — and begins with a few seconds of introductory music. Following the music, Miles welcomes his listeners and says, "Today's diary entry is. . .. " That is the student's clue to listen. Miles will then read the headline title and the content of the story exactly as it is printed on the student's copy of the diary entry.

For many struggling readers, being able to listen to the story first can be extremely beneficial. Knowing the story's content ahead of time provides students with the opportunity of using context clues to help decode words and for interpreting the meaning of the story. For other students, being able to track the text as they listen to the words allows for a multi-sensory experience. Students can hear the words; see the words; and can touch each word as they follow along while listening to each of Mile's exciting mysteries.

About the Activity Pages

Paper and pencil tasks are often "not fun" for struggling readers. The majority of the reproducible activity pages are divided into two different activities per page. The teacher may choose to assign both halves at once. The diversity of the two different activities should encourage the children to finish the page and not become bored or frustrated. The teacher may also choose to cut the page in two and assign each half at different times.

Coloring, drawing, solving puzzles, and cutting and pasting activities have been included. These types of activities reinforce a wide range of reading skills and are often viewed as "more fun" by the students.

In short, *High Interest/Low Readability: Miles Masters' Mystery Diaries* will provide your students with a complete reading experience.

Contents

Miles Masters' Mystery Diaries

From: Miles Masters
Entry: #1
Date: September

Subject: Mystery Magnet

Hi. I'm Miles — Miles Masters. Welcome to my diary. I'm not a very exciting person. I like to read. I like to watch TV. I also like to be in bed by 9:00 pm, but that hardly ever happens. You see, I am a mystery magnet. I just can't help it. I don't go looking for mysteries. The mysteries just come to me.

I might be doing my homework or reading a book. Then suddenly — bam! There it is — a mystery that will need solving. My mind starts buzzing. Questions keep leaping into my brain. I just have to find the answer. I can't sleep! I can't eat! I can't watch TV! I can't even play my video games. I just have to find the answer.

Once I have found one answer, it usually makes me ask another question. And another. And another.

I keep asking questions until I get to the last big question. The last question that will finally solve the mystery.

What else do you need to know about me? Let's see. I live with my Mom and Dad. They are quite old to have a kid my age. But they act like they are young. They love all kinds of sports and outdoor activities. *(I don't.)* They like loud music. *(I don't.)*

I don't have any pets. I don't have any brothers or sisters. And I don't have a girlfriend! *(I'm only 12 years old.)*

My best friend is Matt Kitson. He does not talk very much. He likes to read comic books. And he can play any kind of sport. I like him a lot.

I keep this diary because it helps me to think. It will also help you to understand what it's like to be a mystery magnet.

Enjoy my mystery diaries!
                    Miles

Name _____

Directions: Choose the correct word from the Word Bank to complete each sentence.

Word Bank: music   bed   read   Matt   Miles   outdoor   TV

1. _____ Masters is a mystery magnet.

2. Miles goes to _____ at 9 o'clock.

3. Miles likes to _____ books and watch _____ .

4. Miles' best friend is _____ Kitson.

5. Miles' parents like _____ activities and loud

   _____ .

Directions: Pretend you are Miles Masters.
Draw and color a small poster that shows Miles as a mystery magnet.

Name _____

Directions: Read the sentences at the bottom of the page.
Cut them out along the dotted lines and glue each sentence under the matching picture.

Miles likes to read books.

Miles likes to watch TV.

Miles' parents act like they are young.

Matt Kitson is Miles' best friend.

Miles Masters' Mystery Diaries

From: Miles Masters
Entry: #2
Date: January 2 – 7

Subject: The Missing Dog!

January 2nd

Mr. Brumble's dog has vanished! Mr. Brumble is our neighbor. His dog is named Wolf. *(That should give you a pretty good clue as to what his dog looks like.)* He is huge. His bark is loud. His growl is — well — it's scary.

Mr. Brumble loves Wolf like a baby. He is such a nice man. I have never told him that his dog scares me.

We know that Wolf was in the yard at 2:00 pm today. He growled at me when I left the house. By 2:15, when Mr. Brumble got home, Wolf was gone!

January 3rd

I have spent the day listening to Mr. Brumble talk about Wolf. I now know:
- Wolf loves home-made cakes and breads.
- Wolf has never hurt anyone. *(Even if he looks and sounds like a werewolf.)*
- Wolf is scared of mice and thunder.
- Wolf sleeps on the end of Mr. Brumble's bed. He keeps Mr. Brumble's feet warm.
- Wolf likes to chase dogs and rabbits. He wants to be friends with them. *(Yeah, right!)*

January 4th

Wolf has been gone for three days. There are big problems at home. Mom saw a mouse in her bedroom. She put a trap down. "Shame," I said, "Mice are so cute."

I was brushing my teeth when I thought there might be a link between the mouse and Wolf.

January 5th

I knew it! Mr. Brumble has mice too! "At least Wolf isn't here. He would have run a mile..." said Mr. Brumble. Then he realized what he'd said.

Maybe Wolf ran away from the mice. We still do not know where Wolf went.

January 6th

Four days and still no Wolf. I went to get bagels for Mom this morning. It was lucky I was feeling helpful. If I hadn't gone, I would have missed the biggest clue yet!

"Sorry Miles. We have run out of bagels," said Mrs. Brown. "Twelve bagels in a bag vanished from the back room! I cannot understand it. It's a mystery."

Wolf likes bakery food! This could be good news. He might be nearby.

January 7th

I walked all around the neighborhood with Mr. Brumble and a bag of warm bagels. Mr. Brumble called Wolf's name. I waved the bagels in the air so Wolf might smell them.

There is an old shed in the park at the edge of our neighborhood. As we passed it, there was a scraping sound. The door opened and out jumped Wolf! Wolf ran up and licked Mr. Brumble. Mr. Brumble hugged and stroked Wolf.

We all walked back home, but Wolf would not go in the house. "Does he think the mice are still in the house?" I asked Mr. Brumble.

Wolf was thin. He had not eaten for days. Mr. Brumble held a warm bagel in front of Wolf's nose. After a while, Wolf followed Mr. Brumble and the bagel inside the house. Mr. Brumble led Wolf into every room by holding a bagel by Wolf's nose. This helped show Wolf that the mice were all gone.

I am glad for Mr. Brumble that Wolf is back. But I still would not want to meet Wolf on a dark night.

Name _____

Directions: Read each sentence about the story. Write a "**T**" on the blank if the sentence is true. Write an "**F**" on the blank if the sentence is false.

1. Wolf loves homemade cakes and breads. _____

2. Wolf is not scared of thunder or mice. _____

3. Wolf has never hurt anyone. _____

4. Wolf sleeps on Mr. Brumble's bed. _____

5. Rabbits like to chase Wolf. _____

6. Wolf likes to chase other dogs. _____

Reading for Details

Directions: Draw a line from the date (**Column A**) to the sentence that describes what happened on that day (**Column B**).

Column A   ## Column B

1. January 2   a. Miles' mom saw a mouse in the house.

2. January 3   b. Bagels vanished from the bakery.

3. January 4   c. Wolf has vanished.

4. January 5   d. Wolf was found in a shed in the park.

5. January 6   e. Miles spent the day listening to Mr. Brumble talk about Wolf.

6. January 7   f. Mr. Brumble has mice in his house.

Name _____

Directions: Circle the words from the Word Bank in the word search.
The words may be horizontal or vertical.

M	i	l	e	s	a	l	a	c	e	d
a	a	p	B	r	u	m	b	l	e	i
s	e	h	d	i	n	g	a	m	z	a
t	t	i	z	m	d	o	g	d	c	r
e	r	d	n	i	e	x	e	e	h	y
r	f	e	o	c	W	o	l	f	x	e
s	c	a	r	e	d	e	s	t	e	r
c	r	k	c	l	u	e	s	u	k	w

Word Bank
bagel
Masters
Miles
diary
dog
Brumble
scared
Wolf
hide
mice
clues

Directions: Draw a picture of Wolf sitting in the shed.

Miles Masters' Mystery Diaries

From: Miles Masters
Entry: #3
Date: March 15 – 21

Subject: Socknapped!

> Here is a mystery I solved for my friend Matt.
> I solved it through e-mail.

March 15th

Hi Miles,

Bet you haven't missed me. My grandparents are great. They let me read my comic books all day long. They don't make me go for walks, or go to the mall with them. My mom always makes me go to the mall with her. They are so happy that I am staying with them. They let me e-mail my friends — that's you Miles. But I have a problem. Can you help me?

Matt

Hi Matt,

Thanks for the e-mail. Good news that you get to read comic books all day. I do kind of miss you. You don't say much, but you have a good pair of ears.

So, what's your problem? And why didn't you tell me in your e-mail?

Miles

March 16th

Yo Miles,

Sorry! I guess I'm used to you asking me questions before I say anything. So here is the thing. Someone comes into my room each night and steals my socks. I only have one pair left, so I am keeping them on my feet. They are pretty smelly now and I still have 5 days left here. It's a bad feeling not knowing who is doing it, or why. Any ideas?

Matt

Hi Matt,

I think it's your grandmother! I bet she has put them in the wash.

Miles

March 17th

Hi Miles,
No! It's not her or my grandfather.
Matt

Hi Matt,
How can you be so sure?
Miles

March 18th

Hi Miles,
a. I've asked my grandparents and they both said no.
b. They don't come up to my room. It's in the attic and the stairs are too steep. I have to change the sheets on my bed and everything. Hurry up and work this out. I need my socks.
Matt

Hi Matt,
You are not helping me very much. Give me more clues! Have the socks been kicked under the bed? Does anyone else come into the house? Are you sure they are not in the laundry? Where did you put them when you took them off? This is crazy. I'd be having kittens if it was happening to me.
Miles

March 19th

Hey Miles,
Funny you should say that. Grandma's cat has just had some.
Matt

Hello Matt,
Just had what?
Miles

Hi Miles,
The cat had kittens.
Matt

Matt,
What are they like?
Miles

Hi Miles,

I don't know. They are in the garage. I don't like animals. They trigger my asthma. When I first got here the cat was asleep in my room. She made me wheezy. Grandma called her downstairs but she kept sneaking back up to my room. When she was ready to have the kittens she went back to the garage.

Matt

March 20th

Matt,

Go and have a look at those kittens. Just once. Take your inhaler.

Miles

Hi Miles,

I don't want to.

Matt

Go Matt!
Trust me! I've got a hunch.

Miles

March 21st

Hey Miles,

You're a genius!

Matt

Thank you, Matt.

I do seem to be a genius, don't I? What did you see?

Miles

Hi Miles,

Kittens, very warm and snuggled up in my socks! I told Grandma. She said it's not just birds that build nests for their babies.

Matt

Directions: Read each sentence. In your own words write what you think each sentence means.

_____

- -

_____

2. "I'd be having kittens if it was happening to me."

_____

- -

_____

3. "It's not just birds that build nests for their babies."

_____

- -

_____

Cause and Effect

Directions: A **cause** tells why something has happened and an **effect** tells what happened. Draw a line from each cause in **Column A** to its matching effect in **Column B**.

<u>Column A</u>	<u>Column B</u>
1. Matt's socks are smelly because,	a. she can't walk up the steep stairs to the attic.
2. Matt does not like animals because,	b. she wanted them to make a bed for her babies.
3. Matt's grandma could not have taken his socks because,	c. he will not take them off his feet.
4. The cat took the socks because,	d. they trigger his asthma.

Drawing Conclusions

Directions: Read the question in each box. Write your answer in each speech bubble.

1. What could Matt be thinking about?

2. What could Miles be writing to Matt?

3. What do you think Matt is saying to his grandma?

4. What could Matt be thinking about?

Miles Masters' Mystery Diaries

From: Miles Masters
Entry: #4
Date: April 7–9

Subject: # The Haunted Restroom!

April 7th

They knocked me right over! Two 4th grade girls came running out of the girls' restroom — screaming!

"What's up?" I asked, but they were gone. I'm a boy, so there was no way I could go in there.

I waited for some more girls to go into the restroom. The same thing happened. The girls went in the restroom happy. Then there were screams, banging doors, and out they ran. This time I heard something. There was a deep moaning sound.

I ran after the girls. I found them on the playground.

"What happened in there?" I asked them.

They said, "There's a ghost in our restroom! All the girls have heard it."

"Why do you think it's a ghost?" I asked. *(I was really getting into this.)*

One girl said, "A human could not make that sound. It is too horrible!"

Well, I am Miles Masters and I am not scared. Tomorrow I'm going into the girls' restroom.

April 8th

I knew I would need Matt's help. I found him and said, "Matt. I've got to go into the girl's restroom. You need to stand guard. Make sure that no girls come in."

"Sure," he said. That's why I like him. He doesn't ask any questions.

I went into the girls' restroom and stood still. I waited and waited and waited.

Just silence. I wanted an adventure. I wanted to solve another mystery. I was just about to leave when I heard it. The hairs on the back of my neck stood on end. It was a terrible, terrible sound. And that terrible sound was coming from right behind me. Whatever was making that noise had to be very scary.

I had to turn around and face it. Get ready! One, two, three. I turned around and saw nothing! Nothing. No monster. No ghost.

I did see something else. A metal vent on the wall where the heat comes through. I went closer. This was where the sound was coming from.

Suddenly, it stopped. I stared at the vent and thought for a while.

"Thanks Matt," I said, on my way out.

"No problem," he said.

Tomorrow I'll find the answer to my next question: Where does that vent lead to?

April 9th

Mr. Collins, the school janitor, jumped up when I went into his room.

"Knock before you come in, kid! You wouldn't just walk into the principal's office without knocking, would you?"

I answered, "No, sir."

"What do you want anyway?" asked Mr. Collins.

"Err, my teacher sent me, sir. She wanted me to .. err." *(I should have worked out what I was going to say before I walked in.)*

"Get on with it kid. I have work to do," he said.

So, I replied, "I am working on a project about how sound travels. I am trying to find out…" I glanced over his shoulder.

Something twinkled in the dark.

"What is that, sir?" I asked.

"What's what?" questioned the janitor.

"That gold thing, sir." He looked at me and his face went a little pink.

"I would tell you but it is a secret. Understand, kid?" Mr. Collins said in a firm voice.

I shook my head and said, "Yes, sir."

Mr. Collins finally said, "That gold thing is a tuba — a huge brass musical instrument. I have just started taking lessons. Isn't she a beauty?"

I was pretty sure I was face to face with the girls' restroom ghost. Just to make sure I said, "Mr. Collins, I'd love to hear you play that tuba."

Mr. Collins grinned and picked up the tuba. He sat down on the chair right next to the vent. He puffed out his chest and blew. A long way off I heard a scream.

I imagined all the girls running out of the restroom.

Maybe I will wait a week or two before I tell the girls about Mr. Collins' tuba.

Directions: Read each sentence about the story. Write a "**T**" on the blank if the sentence is true. Write an "**F**" on the blank if the sentence is false.

1.   The girls thought the restroom was haunted by a ghost.   _____

2.   Matt did not stand guard when Miles went into the
     girls' restroom.   _____

3.   At first, Miles was scared when he was in the girls' restroom.   _____

4.   Miles heard a sound coming from under the door.   _____

5.   Miles went to talk to Mr. Atkins about the sounds in
     the restroom.   _____

6.   The scary sounds were Mr. Collins playing the tuba.   _____

Drawing Conclusions

Directions: Why do you think Miles was going to wait a week or two before he told the girls that the scary sound was Mr. Collins playing the tuba?

_____

- -

_____

- -

_____

- -

_____

- -

_____

Directions: Choose a word from the Word Bank to answer each crossword clue.
Write the answers in the correct word boxes.

Word Bank
restroom   in
Miles   ran
tuba   ghost

ACROSS

2. The sound came from the girls' _____.

5. Girls went _____ happy and came out screaming.

6. The girls _____ out of the restroom.

DOWN

1. The girls thought a _____ was in the restroom.

3. The scary sound was a _____.

4. _____ Masters solved the mystery.

Directions: **Antonyms** are two different words that have the opposite meaning. For example, "hot" and "cold" would be antonyms. Draw a line from each word in **Column A** to its matching antonym in **Column B**.

Column A

loud

girl

happy

scared

in

walk

Column B

brave

out

quiet

run

boy

sad

Miles Masters' Mystery Diaries

From: Miles Masters
Entry: #5
Date: May 2–5

Subject: # Near Tragedy at Track and Field Day

May 2nd

I'm not very good at sports or any other outdoor activities. Matt is great. He doesn't even have to try. He can run fast, throw long, and catch well. I don't know how he does it.

"It's a gift," I say to him. "No, it's not," he says back. "Playing sports is easy."

"How come I can't do it?" I ask him.

"You are just too busy being so smart," Matt answered.

Track and Field Day is in three days. It's Matt's one chance to shine. He could win almost everything. *(I won't win anything!)*

May 4th

Track and Field Day is tomorrow. Matt is excited. He really wants to do well. I tell him that he is sure to win.

"Want to bet?" said a voice behind us. Matt didn't hear. But I heard it—it was Luke Walker. Like Matt, Luke is very good at sports. But unlike Matt, Luke is a bad loser.

I am worried that Luke is planning something bad. I must keep a close eye on both Matt and Luke.

May 5th - Track and Field Day

At our school, everyone has to take part in at least one event. I do the long jump because you do not have to race against someone. So, it is not as obvious when you come in last. Also, it's not dangerous, like jumping hurdles, or the high jump. You can fall over the bars in those events.

Matt was doing the high jump, the hurdles, the 100– and the 400– yard dash, and the relay. Luke Walker was in the exact same events.

On my way to school, I saw Luke in the park. He had a yellow glove on one hand. He was putting leaves in his pocket. When he left the park, I walked over to where he had been.

I looked around and saw what I needed to see. Then I quickly collected my own leaves. Luke is a mean nasty person!

We had class for an hour before the events were to begin. I walked past Luke's desk. I saw something yellow and rubbery sticking out of his pocket. I pulled it out and waved it around.

"What's this, Luke? Are you going to wash the dishes?" It was a rubber glove.

People started laughing and Luke got very mad at me. "Give it back, now!" He grabbed the glove and pushed me hard. I fell back on a chair.

Five minutes before we had to get changed for Track and Field Day, Luke said he needed to go to the restroom. I knew he was up to something. He was already changed by the time we got to the locker room.

Outside we were told to warm up. Matt started hopping and was making a strange face. He sat down and pulled off his running shoes. Then he yanked off his socks. They were full of stinging nettles.

"I knew it," I said. "It was Luke. He put stinging nettles in your socks. He wore the rubber glove so he wouldn't get stung."

I started to rub Matt's feet with the leaves I had in my pockets.

Matt looked very surprised, "What are you doing?"

"These leaves will stop the stinging. They always grow next to the nettles," I told Matt.

"Thanks," said Matt. "But if you knew Luke was going to do this, why didn't you stop him?"

"Because I want him to get into trouble. He has to stop being so mean."

I came in last in the long jump. Matt was first in everything, except the high jump. Luke won that event, which is kind of funny. When we told our teacher that Luke had put stinging nettles in Matt's socks, our teacher said, "That boy is in for tall trouble!"

Directions: Circle **yes** or **no** for each sentence.

1.   At the park, Miles puts leaves in his pockets.   **yes**   **no**

2.   Miles saw Luke with a blue glove.   **yes**   **no**

3.   Miles Masters does the long jump.   **yes**   **no**

4.   Luke Walker is a bad loser.   **yes**   **no**

5.   Matt won every event.   **yes**   **no**

6.   Track and Field Day was on May 4th.   **yes**   **no**

Directions: Circle the words from the Word Bank in the word search.
The words may be horizontal or vertical.

```
t  r  a  c  k  a  M  a  t  t  f
a  s  t  i  n  g  i  n  g  e  i
s  c  h  d  i  n  l  L  u  k  e
t  h  i  z  j  d  e  g  d  c  l
l  o  n  g  u  e  s  e  e  h  d
r  o  e  o  m  w  o  x  f  x  e
s  l  a  r  p  w  i  n  n  e  r
n  e  t  t  l  e  s  s  u  k  w
```

Word Bank
track
Luke
Miles
Matt
stinging
nettles
school
winner
long
jump

Name _____

Directions: Look at the pictures at the bottom of the page.
Cut them out along the dotted lines and glue them in the correct order.

1	2
3	4

-28- *Miles Masters' Mystery Diaries*

Miles Masters' Mystery Diaries

From: Miles Masters
Entry: #6
Date: May 10–14

Subject: # The Headless Teacher

May 10th

I am in big trouble with my teacher, Miss Pith. Being a mystery magnet, I get into trouble all the time. But what can I do?

Miss Pith asked me to go to the classroom next door and get a pen from Mrs. Mull. Then she got mad at me because I came back without the pen. I just couldn't tell Miss Pith why. I kept my mouth shut and she got angry with me. Tomorrow I cannot go out at recess — just because I was being kind to Miss Pith.

You see, when I went to Mrs. Mull's classroom it was empty. The class was outside at recess. On her desk was a pile of photos. There were photos of school plays, school parties, track and field days, and many other school events. My blood ran cold. In every single photo Miss Pith's face had been cut out. It was horrible!

Where were all of Miss Pith's faces? Why had Mrs. Mull cut them out?

"Get out of there, Miles! What do you think you are doing? This is private," yelled Mrs. Mull. She had come back into the room. She ran over to the desk and stuffed all the photos in a bag. Then she put the bag under her desk. I left in a hurry and forgot to ask for the pen.

Does Mrs. Mull hate Miss Pith? Is she going to scare her with those nasty cut-up photos? I've got detention with Miss Pith tomorrow. I will try then to find out more about her and Mrs. Mull.

May 11th

Something is wrong. I just don't know what. During detention I helped Miss Pith put up a wall display. She didn't seem angry with me, so I thought it was safe to start my detective work.

"So, Miss Pith, do you like teaching here?" I asked.

She gave me a look that could have been sad, or it could have been angry. She replied, "Why do you ask, Miles?"

"I was wondering what it's like. Are you friends with the other teachers?"

"Yes, Miles. All of the teachers are really great friends. It's just a pity . . ." Then her voice became shaky. "Excuse me, Miles," she said and rushed out of the room.

I think Miss Pith is being bullied by Mrs. Mull.

May 12th

Terrible news! Miss Pith told us she's leaving the school! It must be because Mrs. Mull was cutting up those photos of her.

May 13th

It's worse than I thought!

Mrs. Mull was joking with Miss Pith in the hall. Poor Miss Pith doesn't even know that Mrs. Mull is doing these nasty things to her. I must put a stop to this.

At the end of the school day, Mrs. Mull was alone in her room.

"Mrs. Mull," I said, calmly. "I know what you are doing to Miss Pith. I saw the photos and I am going to tell the principal."

Mrs. Mull laughed and said, "He already knows Miles. He's the one who asked me to do it!" What do I do now? Oh no! The school is run by a bully!

May 14th

How dumb am I? This was the most embarrassing day of my whole life!

Mr. Atkins, our principal, told the school that Miss Pith was leaving. "Miss Pith is leaving to become the principal of her own school. We are very sad to see her go. She has been an excellent teacher."

I know I shouldn't have done what I did next. But it made me mad to hear Mr. Atkins saying nice things about Miss Pith when he was really being so mean. I didn't plan it! One minute I was sitting on the floor and the next minute I was standing up and shouting, "She's only leaving because of you!"

Miss Pith said, "Miles!" her voice was all squeaky. I thought she would be pleased with me. But Miss Pith did not look at all pleased.

"Miles, sit down right now," said Mr. Atkins. "I will deal with you after I have finished." Mr. Atkins was very stern.

People were giggling and looking at me. I glared at Mr. Atkins. He carried on with his speech.

"To show everyone what a star we think Miss Pith is, her good friend Mrs. Mull has made her something special."

Mr. Atkins took out a huge poster with Miss Pith's face stuck on all of these famous people's bodies, like Madonna, Rocky, and King Kong. It was really funny. At the top, in huge letters, it said, "Miss Pith, the Star of Greenway School."

I told Mr. Atkins and Miss Pith that I was sorry. I told them about my mistake. Mr. Atkins said I had to stay in at recess for being rude in assembly. Miss Pith patted me on the back after he had left.

Note to myself – things are not always what they seem.

Name _____

Directions: A **fact** is something that is true. An **opinion** is something that a person thinks, believes, or feels. Write the word "**fact**" or the word "**opinion**" next to each sentence.

_____   1.   Miss Pith's face was cut out of many photos.

_____   2.   Mrs. Mull thinks Miss Pith is pretty.

_____   3.   During detention Miles helped Miss Pith put up a wall display.

_____   4.   The school is run by a bully.

_____   5.   Miss Pith is leaving Miles' school to become the principal at another school.

Creative Writing

Directions: Pretend you are Miles Masters.
What two questions would you ask Mrs. Mull?

_____

- -

_____

_____

- -

_____

_____

- -

_____

_____

- -

Name _____

Directions: Design a poster about your teacher.

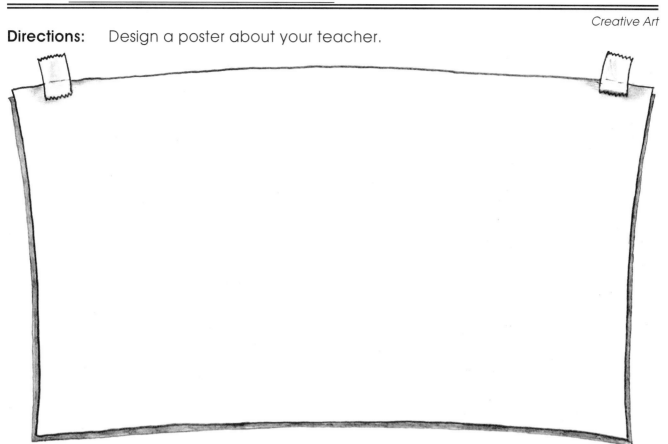

Directions: Choose the correct word from the Word Bank to complete each sentence.

Word Bank:	**face**	**bully**	**photos**	**yells**	**school**	**Mrs. Mull**

1.   Miles saw _____ on Mrs. Mull's desk.

2.   Miss Pith's _____ was cut out of all the photos!

3.   Miles thinks that _____ is not Miss Pith's friend.

4.   Miles thinks that Mr. Atkins is a _____.

5.   Miles _____ during a school assembly.

6.   Miles learns that Miss Pith is leaving his _____ to become a principal at another school.

Name _____

Directions: The **main idea** tells what the story is about. Read the following sentences and circle the sentence that you think best explains the main idea of the story.

1. Miles thinks that Mrs. Mull and Mr. Atkins are bullies.

2. Miles gets in trouble all the time.

3. Miles wants to solve the mystery of why Miss Pith's face was cut out of the photos.

Sequence

Directions: Look at the pictures below. Cut them out along the dotted lines and glue them in sequential order.

1.	2.	3.

 Miles Masters' Mystery Diaries

Miles Masters' Mystery Diaries

From: Miles Masters
Entry: #7
Date: June 9–15

Subject: One Mean Teacher

June 9th

Mr. Perry is one mean teacher! I know you can't like everyone and everyone can't like you. But Mr. Perry seems to hate everyone. And because of that, everyone seems to hate Mr. Perry. I wish Miss Pith would come back!

Here is a list of some of the mean things Mr. Perry has done during his first week at our school:

- He shouted so loud at Carla Matthews that she cried. All she did was drop her pen on the floor.
- He scolded Ben Hollins for getting 100% on the science test. Mr. Perry said he was just showing off!
- He kept John Glover in every lunchtime for a whole week because Mr. Perry said he could smell his tuna sandwich when he walked past his desk.

Everyone is complaining about Mr. Perry. I've been thinking. I believe there is a pattern.

- He punishes the smart kids when all they have done is work hard.
- He goes crazy if anyone makes a noise when the class is quiet.
- He gives the class detention if anyone brings something smelly into the classroom.

I have a theory. I need to check it out.

June 10th

Today Matt was given extra homework after he got 100% on the math test.

June 11th

I dropped my ruler on the floor during silent reading. Mr. Perry shouted so loudly that Mr. Atkins put his head in the door to see if we were all okay.

June 12th

I brought a chunk of Dad's blue cheese to school. It smells horrible! I kept it in my pocket all day so it would really smell bad. Now everyone has to miss recess for a week.

Everyone is mad at me now, but they will thank me in the end.

So, now I have my next mystery: Why is Mr. Perry so mean?

June 13th

Major clues! On my way to lunch, I saw Mr. Perry in the hall. He was frowning at one of the old school photos on the bulletin board. He looked unhappy when he walked away. I went over and looked at the photo. The picture was of a class from 20 years ago. One of the kid's names was Perry! I looked closely at the boy who was my age. At first it didn't look at all like Mr. Perry. But then I saw that his nose had the same shape. I also saw that his eyebrows met in the middle, just like Mr. Perry's.

Mr. Perry was a student here! Why didn't he tell us? Maybe he has a secret to keep.

My next surprise was to find out that his teacher was Mr. Atkins, our principal. Only Mr. Atkins looked much younger in the photos.

Then I found another clue after lunch. Mr. Perry was yelling at Beth Stone for staring out the window. That was so unfair! She had finished all of her work long ago.

"Being smart does not mean that you can't be punished Beth. I should know," yelled Mr. Perry.

Tomorrow I need to ask Mr. Atkins, our principal, some questions.

June 14th

"Sir, we are doing interviews with members of the school staff. Can I talk to you about when you first started teaching?" I asked Mr. Atkins during recess.

"Well Miles, you may be surprised to know at first I didn't think I was cut out for teaching."

"Why, sir?" I asked.

Mr. Atkins explained, "Because of my ears and nose, Miles."

I had to ask, "What about your ears and nose, sir?"

"Ever since I was a small boy I have had a super strong sense of smell and hearing. I don't mean to be rude Miles, but you young people can be kind of smelly and noisy. But in time, I got used to the smells and noises."

"But that wasn't my only problem, Miles. I was young and afraid of losing control of the classroom. I gave far too many punishments. I was far too strict," Mr. Atkins explained.

"What was the worst thing you did, sir?" I asked.

"I was much too hard on the smart kids. I worried they would give me the most trouble. Like poor Mr. Perry — I bet you didn't know that he was in my class the very first year I taught here," Mr. Atkins said.

"He was a very smart student, but I gave him such a hard time. I'm ashamed to say it, but I was worried that he was smarter than me!" continued Mr. Atkins.

Mr. Atkins went on to say, "But in time, I saw the best way to get kids to work hard was to like them. I am a very different teacher now than I was then, Miles. Still, I wish I could tell my first students that I am sorry."

"Like Mr. Perry?" I asked.

"Yes, exactly like Mr. Perry," said Mr. Atkins.

"But you could tell him that you are sorry, couldn't you, sir?" I asked hopefully.

"It is too late now, Miles. What would be the point?" wondered Mr. Atkins.

"My Mom says that it is never too late to say you are sorry. It's worth a try," I said.

"Maybe I will do that, Miles. Maybe I will," said Mr. Atkins as he walked away.

"Please tell him, sir. Tell him everything you told me. I think he will be interested."

June 15th

I dropped my book on the floor during silent reading.

Mr. Perry didn't even look up! I wonder . . .

Name _____

Directions: Look at the pictures at the bottom of the page.
Cut them out along the dotted lines and glue them in the correct order.

1	2
3	4

Name _____

Directions: Choose a word from the Word Bank to answer each crossword clue. Write the answers in the correct word boxes.

Word Bank: principal Miles stern lesson sorry Perry

ACROSS

2. Mr. Atkins is the _____.

4. Mr. Perry is _____.

5. Mr. Atkins should say "I'm _____

DOWN

1. _____ solves mysteries.

2. Miles' teacher is Mr. _____.

3. Even a teacher can learn a _____.

Directions: Read the word boxes at the bottom of the page. Which words describe Mr. Perry? Which words describe Mr. Atkins? Which words can be used to describe both of the men? Cut out the word boxes along the dotted lines and glue them into the correct section of the Venn diagram.

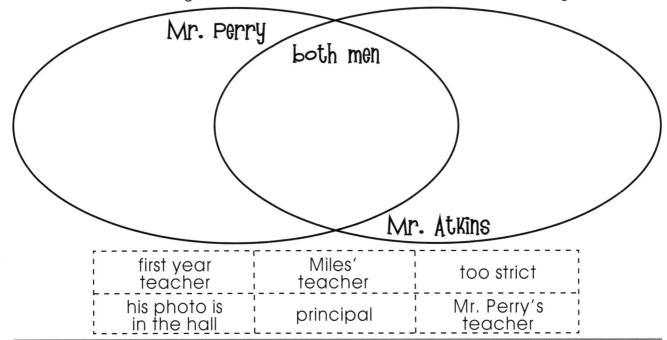

Mr. Perry   both men   Mr. Atkins

| first year teacher | Miles' teacher | too strict |
| his photo is in the hall | principal | Mr. Perry's teacher |

Miles Masters' Mystery Diaries

From: Miles Masters
Entry: #8
Date: July 6 – 20

Subject: # The Dangerous Vacation

July 6th

My parents are great, but they are old. They are as old as Matt's grandparents! Matt's parents are really young. The funny thing is — my parents act as if they are young. On vacation we always have to do something exciting like rock climbing or scuba diving.

When Matt's family goes on vacation they take lots of books. When they get there, they just sit and read. If they feel like it, they might go swimming.

Matt and I think we were swapped at birth. I should be the one reading and swimming and Matt should be rock climbing.

This is day 1 of our tree walking vacation. Tree walking! My parents think it's fun to put our lives at risk. How I wanted to just sit and read. The only thing to worry about would be dripping ice cream onto my book!

Today I climbed rope ladders up onto tiny platforms. I was 50 feet up in the air. I walked on a tight rope over to a tiny platform on the next tree. Then I hurled myself down to the ground on a zip wire. Then I did it all over again — 5 times! My arms hurt and my knees are still wobbling.

I can see one of the tree platforms from my window. It's so high up!

Oh, I see our teacher, Jack. He's wearing a hat and a long coat. I can tell it's him because he walks with a small limp.

He is hiding something in the bushes below the zip wire. I wonder what it is.

No tree walking tomorrow *(thank goodness)*! There's a safety inspection. At least we will know that the wires are safe.

July 7th

The wires are not safe! The Tree Walking Center has failed the inspection! We will get our money back and no more tree walking **(yea!)**. We were told that we could go home or that we could use their bikes free of charge. We could go bike riding in the forest for the rest of the week.

I was riding to the store when I saw the owner of the Center talking to one of the teachers. I slowed down as I passed. "There's no way that wire was broken. I checked it at the end of the day. Someone must have messed with it," he said.

I told you I was a mystery magnet. Here is another mystery for me to solve.

Back in my room, I saw Jack again from my window. He was on his cell phone. He was laughing and laughing. Why is he so happy if the Center has just failed the safety test? Then he started looking for something in the bushes. After 5 minutes he left. He didn't find what he was looking for. I'm going out to have a look around.

I found what Jack was looking for in the bushes. I took it and now it's in my room! It was a bag with a flashlight and a mini-saw in it. Jack must have gone up after dark and cut the zip wire. Then he left the bag in the bushes. Then that stupid man couldn't remember where he left the bag! But why would he do that?

I have an idea, but I need to have a friendly talk with Jack first.

July 8th

I followed Jack into the room where we eat breakfast. I put on my saddest, almost crying face. Then I said to Jack, "I am so fed up. All I have ever wanted to do is tree walk. Now I won't ever be able to do it. This is the only place to do it for miles. My parents don't like to travel very far."

Jack looked around the room. He put his face very close to mine and said, "You must not tell anyone."

"I am opening my own place near here. It is a lot like this Center, but much better. I will give you a special deal. Here is a paper telling all about my place. Don't show it to your parents until you get home."

"Creep!" I thought.

I think it is time to give Jack's bag to his boss. I will add a note.
I wrote: "I found this in the forest. Ask Jack what it was doing there? Also ask him about his new job."

July 11th
No Jack. I went for lots of bike rides and canoe rides. I had a lot of fun staying on the ground.

July 20th
Headlines in the paper: **Tree Walking Center Teacher Arrested for Cutting a Zip Wire!**

The Center will re-open in two weeks. We got a voucher for a free weekend there. Mom and Dad are thrilled. Me? I am not so sure.

Directions: A **cause** tells why something has happened and an **effect** tells what happened. Draw a line from each cause in **Column A** to its matching effect in **Column B**.

Column A

1. Miles' parents love going on exciting vacations because,

2. Matt's parents may be young but they like the quiet because,

3. Miles thought Jack was getting into some trouble because,

4. The Tree Walking Center will reopen because,

Column B

a. he saw Jack hide something in the bushes.

b. they love to act young.

c. Jack was caught and will now go to jail.

d. they love to sit and read.

Directions: Read each question. Circle the picture that answers each question.

1. What did Miles want to do on vacation?

3. What two things were in Jack's bag?

2. What did Miles do after the Center failed the inspection?

4. What happened to Jack?

Name _____

Directions: Look at each of the pictures. Write a sentence about what you think is happening in each of the pictures.

_____
- -
_____
_____
- -
_____

_____
- -
_____
_____
- -
_____

_____
- -
_____
_____
- -
_____

Name _____

Directions: Circle the words from the Word Bank in the word search.
The words may be horizontal or vertical.

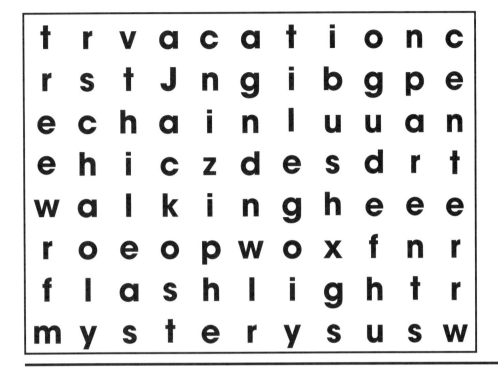

t	r	v	a	c	a	t	i	o	n	c
r	s	t	J	n	g	i	b	g	p	e
e	c	h	a	i	n	l	u	u	a	n
e	h	i	c	z	d	e	s	d	r	t
w	a	l	k	i	n	g	h	e	e	e
r	o	e	o	p	w	o	x	f	n	r
f	l	a	s	h	l	i	g	h	t	r
m	y	s	t	e	r	y	s	u	s	w

Word Bank
tree
walking
zip
center
vacation
mystery
flashlight
Jack
parents
bush

Directions: Circle **yes** or **no** for each sentence.

1. Matt's family brings lots of books on their vacations.   **yes**   **no**

2. Miles' parents enjoy exciting vacations.   **yes**   **no**

3. Miles was on a platform a 100 feet high.   **yes**   **no**

4. Jack found the person who cut the zip wire.   **yes**   **no**

5. Jack wanted to start his own Tree Walking Center.   **yes**   **no**

6. Miles found the flashlight and saw that Jack hid
in the bushes.   **yes**   **no**

Miles Masters' Mystery Diaries

From: Miles Masters
Entry: #9
Date: August 17 – 21

Subject: Teleporting!

August 17th

Matt's cousin has come to visit. I never even knew he had one. Matt doesn't tell me much.

He is mad at me because the girl he likes (Hillary Walker) told him she thinks I'm cute! He shouldn't be mad at me because:

1. I don't like Hillary Walker.
2. Matt does, but he never speaks to her!
3. It's not my fault that girls think I'm cute.

Matt's sister says that girls like me because I'm small and geeky. Matt laughs when his sister says that. I think girls like me because I look like a young Will Smith. Tomorrow I get to meet Matt's cousin.

August 18th

I met Matt's cousin! I have so many questions. My brain feels frozen.

Think clearly. What happened?

I met Matt's cousin — Louise. Matt's cousin is a girl! She smiled a lot and she is very pretty. She has long brown hair and blue eyes. She said, "Hi Miles. It is nice to meet you." A flash of blue from her ring sparkled when she tossed her hair back.

Miles said I could borrow his new comic book. He told me I could go upstairs and get it. "Hurry back, Miles," said Louise, smiling at me.

I ran upstairs, tripped over two suitcases, and fell into Matt's room. There she was again! Sitting on Matt's bed holding the comic book.

"Hi Miles, what kept you?" she asked, as her ring sparkled red.

"Louise! How did you do that?" I sputtered.

The phone rang. "Miles," Matt called from downstairs. "Your mom wants you at home right now. She says it's urgent."

"How did you do that?" I asked again.

"Don't you need to go?" she asked.

I ran downstairs and out the door. My heart was thumping.

When I got home, I yelled, "Mom. I'm home. What is it?"

"There is someone here to see you, Miles. Go into the den," said Mom.

I got a sick feeling in my stomach because I knew what was going to happen. I walked into the den — there she was sitting on the sofa.

"Hi Miles," said Louise. I then pinched my arm. It hurt. I wasn't dreaming.

My Mom gave her a drink and sat with us. I couldn't ask how she learned to teleport. Not with my Mom in the room. She kept smiling at me and stroking her hair. Her ring was flashing blue in the sunshine.

Finally she left. I tried calling Matt on the phone, but he said he couldn't talk. I'm freaked out. Louise could appear at any time or any place.

August 19th

Matt's family have all gone out for the day. That gives me a chance to work things out. People can't teleport! That is impossible. But how does she move from place to place so fast? At least I have found two important clues.

August 20th

Miles Masters, Mystery Magnet — I am a total genius!

This morning I knocked on Matt's door. If I was wrong, I was about to look pretty stupid, but if I was right . . .

Matt opened the door.

"Hi Matt, want to hang out this morning?" I asked.

"Sure," said Matt. He looked behind him. Then in a loud voice he said, "Come on in Miles. Let's go to my room."

"Is Louise around?" I asked, trying to sound like I didn't really care.

"Matt called her, and after a while she came in.

"Hi Miles," she said. "How are you today?"

I acted as though everything was normal. "I'm good, thanks for asking. Would you like to go for a walk today?"

"Sure." She looked at Matt, "That would be fun. Do you mean just the two of us, Miles?"

"No, it would be much more fun if you bring your sister with you. We could play tricks on people," I answered.

I wish I'd had a camera. You should have seen their faces!

Matt threw his comic book down and asked, "How did you know?"

I explained, "Because people can't be in two places at one time."

"But how could you be so sure?" asked Louise.

I told her that there were two main clues:

1. I fell over two identical suitcases yesterday.
2. The stone in your ring was blue when I met you. Then it was red in Matt's bedroom. Then it was blue again when you were in my house.

The door opened and in walked Leila — Louise's identical twin. "Hi Miles," she smiled.

August 21st

The girls are gone. Matt was grumpy.

"You really had me fooled for a while. I was terrified!" I said to cheer him up.

"Hum," said Matt, reading his comic.

"Sulk then. I can't help being good at working things out."

"It's not that — smart guy."

"What then?" I asked.

"If you must know, Louise and Leila both think you are cute."

Name _____

Drawing Conclusions

Directions: Read the question in each box. Write your answer in each speech bubble.

1. What do you think the twins are saying to each other?

2. What could Miles be thinking?

3. What could Miles be thinking?

4. What do you think Matt is saying to Miles?

Name _____

Directions: Look at each of the characters. Then write a list of words that would describe each of them.

Miles	Matt	The Twins

Name _____

Directions: Choose the correct word from the Word Bank to complete each sentence.

Word Bank:	cousin	blue	two	red	pretty	Leila

1. Louise is Matt's _____ .

2. Miles thought Louise was very _____ .

3. Lousie's ring flashed the color _____ .

4. Later, the ring flashed the color _____ .

5. Miles tripped over _____ suitcases.

6. Louise's sister's name is _____ .

Directions: A **cause** tells why something has happened and an **effect** tells what happened. Draw a line from each cause in **Column A** to its matching effect in **Column B**.

Column A

1. Matt was mad at Miles because,

2. Miles thought Louise could teleport because,

3. Miles first knew Louise was a twin because,

4. Miles also knew the girls were twins because,

Column B

a. one wore a blue ring and one wore a red ring.

b. she seemed to be in two places at once.

c. all the girls think Miles is cute.

d. he fell over two identical suitcases.

Miles Masters' Mystery Diaries

From: Miles Masters
Entry: #10
Date: September 15 – 20

Subject: **Bullied!**

September 15th

There is something wrong with Peter Fisher. Peter is a small, shy kid in my class. The last few weeks he has been even quieter. Too quiet. He comes to school late nearly every day. *(He never used to be late.)* When he comes in — five minutes after the bell — his face is red and he is out of breath.

I watch him closely as he takes off his jacket and gets his books and pens out. His hands shake. You can also see that he would really like to cry. Then he sits down and starts his work. He doesn't talk to anyone all day. Tomorrow I am going to try to talk to him.

September 16th

"Hi Peter," I said at recess, "How's It going?" He just kept reading his book. "I walk past your house on the way to school," I said. "Would you like to walk to school with me? It might help you get to school on time."

"No!" he yelled back at me. He looked scared. You'd think I was a werewolf or something.

September 17th

Today I also got in trouble for being late. I hid around the corner from Peter's house so I could find out what's going on. He came out of his house and looked up and down the street. Then he ran to the little park on the way to our school. He crawled into a large bush.

Ten seconds later he came out, and started running backwards — away from school. I followed him. He ran backwards all the way around the block. He came back to the bush and then he ran to school. Only this time he ran facing the right way.

I tried to talk to him, but when he saw me he stopped and said, "Leave me alone!" I really feel sorry for Peter.

September 18th

I followed him again. He left his house, went to the park, and dove into the same bush. I saw that he had a piece of paper in his hand when he came out. He stuffed the paper in his pocket. He looked angry and upset at the same time. Then he jumped all the way around the block.

Both Peter and I were kept in at recess for being late to school.

I tried to talk to him again when we were sitting outside the principal's office. "I can't seem to get out of bed on time these days. What about you? Why are you always late?" I asked.

"Why can't you just leave me alone?" Peter said in an angry whisper. I wonder if he's crazy.

September 19th

I have to solve this mystery fast. Mr. Perry is getting very upset with me for being late. He said he might have to talk to my parents.

This morning I followed Peter again. Today when he came out of the bush he put the paper in his pocket. Then he started skipping. I knew I had to get that piece of paper from him.

When we were in gym class, I asked if I could go back inside and get a drink of water. I found Peter's jacket and checked the pockets. I found lots of pieces of paper. They all had orders written on them:

- Jump round the block — we're watching you!
- Run backwards and don't fall down.
- Crawl on your hands and knees — we will enjoy watching this.

Poor Peter! Someone is making him do these things. Who? Why? I need to solve this mystery fast. I'm getting into too much trouble for being late. The principal said he will be waiting for us at the school's front door tomorrow.

I have an idea! I must go to bed. I need to be up very early in the morning.

September 20th

I got up at 6:00 am and hid behind a tree in the park. I was spying on the bush where Peter goes in each day. Two high school boys came along. I heard them say, "What shall we make him do today?"

"Run sideways, like a crab?"
"We did that the first week."
"Hopping?"
"Haven't done that one! Excellent."
One of them wrote the order on a piece of paper. They put it in a jar and hid it in the bush. Then one boy said, "We have time to get some candy from the store before he shows up." Then they walked off.

I went into the bush and took the paper. It said, "With your eyes closed — no peeking, hop around the park!"

Peter could get hurt, even killed, I thought. I was angry.

I swapped their note for one I had written that morning. My note said, "No more orders. Just go to school. It's over." Then I hid again.

Peter came along and went into the bush. He came out reading the note. I don't think he could believe it. He looked up and down the street. He started walking. I was scared. I didn't know where the boys were. I knew I had to catch up with Peter before they did.

For the first time in ages Peter smiled and said, "Hi."

The smile fell off his face when we heard a big gruff voice shout, "Hey, Peter! Why are your eyes open? Didn't we say we were watching you?"

They started running after us! "Run, Peter, run!" I shouted.

He looked at me very scared. The boys were faster than we were and caught up with us. But luckily, we all ran right into Mr. Atkins. He was standing at the school's front door.

"What's going on, boys?" he asked.

"Ask them, sir," I said, panting. "They are the reason Peter has been late every day."

Peter was scared. He looked at me and then at the boys who were staring at him.

"It's true, sir," said Peter. "They are bullying me. My older brother had a fight with one of them. They are scared of him, so they pick on me."

The boys didn't look so scary as they went with Mr. Atkins into his office. I'm walking to school with Peter tomorrow. We'll be there early.

Name _____

Directions: Read each sentence about the story. Write a "**T**" on the blank if the
sentence is true. Write an "**F**" on the blank if the sentence is false.

1.   Peter Fisher was being bullied by two big boys.   _____

2.   Miles never got into trouble for being late.   _____

3.   Miles followed Peter on September 17, 18, and 19.   _____

4.   Pieces of paper with "orders" on them were being
     hidden in the bush at the park.   _____

5.   Peter followed the orders after school!   _____

6.   The boys ran into Mr. Atkins at the school's front door.   _____

Creative Writing

Directions: Draw a picture and write a sentence about your favorite part of the story.

Name _____

Directions: In you own words write about why you think the two older boys were bullying Peter.

_ _

_____

_____

_ _

_____

_____

_ _

_____

_____

_ _

_____

Directions: Look at the pictures below. Cut them out along the dotted lines and glue them in sequential order.

1.	2.	3.

High-Frequency, Easy-to-Sound Out, and Special Words for Each Story

a	bird's	done	games	hug	lot	restroom	of
about	blew	don't	gave	huge	loud	riding	off
act	blue	door	get	hurt	love	right	old
added	book	down	gift	I	lucky	room	oldest
after	both	drink	girl	if	lunch	run	on
again	brain	during	give	I'm	mad	sad	once
against	bread	each	glad	in	made	said	one
alive	bring	easy	go	inside	make	saw	only
all	brought	eat	goes	into	makes	say	onto
almost	boy	else	going	is	mall	scared	open
alone	brother	end	gold	isn't	man	school	or
along	build	ended	gone	it	many	see	other
also	bush	enough	good	it's	math	seem	our
am	busy	even	got	jar	may	seem	out
an	but	ever	great	jump	maybe	seen	outdoor
and	by	everyone	grin	jumped	me	shall	outside
angry	cake	everything	ground	just	men	she	over
another	called	face	had	keep	mice	shed	own
answer	calling	fact	hagn't	kept	might	sheets	paper
any	calls	fall	hand	kid	mile	shook	parents
anyone	came	family	hanging	kind	mind	should	park
anything	can	fast	happening	kittens	mine	shouted	part
are	candy	fastest	happy	knew	minute	show	passed
aren't	cans	father	hard	know	missed	side	pen
around	can't	fear	hare	knowing	missing	sign	people
as	carried	fed	has	ladder	mom	silly	person
ask	cat	feel	have	land	moment	since	piece
asked	change	feeling	haven't	large	more	sing	place
asking	chair	feet	he	last	morning	singing	plan
at	class	fell	head	late	most	sir	planning
away	climb	felt	hear	later	mother	sisters	play
babies	climbed	finally	heard	laugh	mouse	sit	please
back	close	find	heart	learn	much	sleeping	pretty
bad	clue	finish	heavy	least	must	sleeps	puffed
bars	come	firm	held	leave	my	slept	pull
be	coming	first	help	left	myself	slow	push
beaten	could	fit	helped	let	name	small	put
beauty	couldn't	five	her	lets	nasty	smart	question
because	crawl	fix	hiding	like	need	smell	quiet
become	cut	followed	high	likes	nest	smile	rabbit
been	dark	for	him	link	never	smiled	race
bed	dad	forget	his	listen	new	snapped	rags
before	day	found	hold	little	next	so	ran
being	deal	free	home	live	nice	soft	read
believe	did	friend	homework	living	night	some	readers
best	died	from	hop	long	no	something	ready
bet	do	front	hope	look	not	sorry	real
between	does	fun	house	looked	nothing	sounds	really
bike	dog	funny	how	lost	now	speak	red
							spent	

spoke
sport
stairs
stand
start
started
steady
steep
still
stop
stopped
stood
store
story
streets
sure
surprised
such
take
talk
talking
tall
teacher
tears
teeth
tell
tells
than
thanks
that
the
their
them
then
there
they
thing
think
this
those
thought
travels
three
threw
thrilled
through
throw
time
tiny
to

today
together
told
tomorrow
too
took
tossed
town
tree
trick
tried
true
trust
try
turn
turned
TV
two
ugly
usually
under
understand
up
upset
upstairs
us
used
vacation
very
wait
waiting
walk
walked
want
wanted
wants
warm
was
wash
watch
wave
way
we
wearing
week
well
went
were
what
whatever

when
where
which
while
white
who
whole
will
win
wire
wish
with
without
woman
women
won
woods
work
worked
worried
would
wrap
wrong
wrote
yard
yelled
yellow
yes
yesterday
you
young
your
you're

Special Words for Each Story

Special Words for Story #1
activities
diary
exciting
girlfriend
leaping
magnet
Matt Kitson
Miles Masters
mystery
solve

Special Words for Story #2
bagels
bakery
edge
growl
Mr. Brumble
neighbor
neighborhood
problems
realized
thunder
vanished
werewolf
Wolf

Special Words for Story #3
asthma
comic books
crazy
e-mail
garage
genius
grandfather
grandmmother
grandparents
laundry

sneaking
Special Words for Story #4
adventure
ghost
human
imagined
janitor
moaning
Mr. Collins
musical instrument
principal
poject
screaming
silence
terrible
tuba
twinkled

Special Words for Story #5
dangerous
event
hurdles
Luke Walker
obvious
stining nettles
Track and Field
yanked

Special Words for Story #6
assembly
dectective
detention
embarrassing
giggling
Miss Pith
mistake
Mr. Atkins
Mrs. Mull
photos
principal
special
stern

Special Words for Story #7
ashamed
bulletin Board
frowning
interviews
Mr. Perry
punishes
scolded
science
silent
strict
theory
unfair

Special Words for Story #8
canoe
cel phone
center
Jack
platform
scuba diving
swapped
swimming

Special Words for Story #9
camera
cousin
Hillary Walker
Lousie
Leila
sparkled
sputtered
suitcases
teleporting
urgent

Special Words for Story #10
backwards
checked
excellent
pocket
recess

Answer Key

Top of page 7
1. Miles; 2. bed; 3. read, TV;
4. Matt; 5. outdoor, music

Bottom of page 7
Check students' work

Page 8
1. Miles likes to watch TV.
2. Miles' parents act like they are young.
3. Matt Kitson is Miles' best friend.
4. Miles likes to read books.

Top of page 12
1. T; 2. F; 3. T; 4. T; 5. F; 6. T

Bottom of page 12
1. c; 2. e; 3. a; 4. f; 5. b; 6. d

Top of page 13
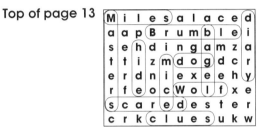

Bottom of page 13
Check students' work

Top of page 17
Check students' work

Bottom of page 17
1. c; 2. d; 3. a; 4. b

Page 18
Check students' work

Top of page 22
1. T; 2. F; 3. T; 4. F; 5. F; 6. T

Bottom of page 22
Check students' work

Top of page 23
Across: 2. restroom; 5. in; 6. ran
Down: 1. ghost; 3. tuba; 4. Miles

Bottom of page 23
loud/quiet;   girl/boy;   happy/sad;
scared/brave;   in/out;   walk/run

Top of page 27
1. yes; 2. no; 3. yes;
4. yes; 5. no 6. no

Bottom of page 27

Page 28
1. Miles is at the park watching Luke stuff his pockets full of leaves.
2. Luke walks away and then Miles picks some leaves.
3. Matt is jumping up and down in pain.
4. Miles is rubbing Matt's feet with leaves to reduce the pain.

Top of page 32
1. fact; 2. opinion; 3. fact; 4. opinion; 5. fact

Bottom of page 32
Check students' work

Top of page 33
Check students' work

Bottom of page 33
1. photos; 2. face; 3. Mrs. Mull;
4. bully; 5. yells: 6. school

Top of page 34
3. Miles wants to solve the mystery of why Miss Pith's face was cut out of the photos.

Bottom of page 34
1. Miles looking at the face-less photos on Mrs. Mull's desk.
2. An upset Miles is talking to Mrs. Mull.
3. Miles is yelling during the school assembly.

Page 39
1. Mr. Perry yelling at his class.
2. Miles talking to Mr. Atkins.
3. Mr. Atkins talking to Mr. Perry.
4. Mr. Perry looking nice and friendly at his class.

Top of page 40
Across: 2. principal; 4. stern; 5. sorry
Down: 1. Miles; 2. Perry; 3. lesson

Bottom of page 40
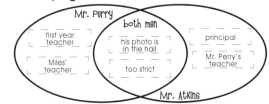

Answer Key

Top of page 45
1. b; 2. d; 3. a; 4. c

Bottom of page 45
1. Miles wanted to read a book.
2. Miles went bike riding.
3. Jack had a flashlight and a mini-saw in his bag.
4. Jack went to jail.

Page 46
Check students' work

Top of page 47

Bottom of page 47
1. yes; 2. yes; 3. no; 4. no; 5. yes; 6. yes

Page 52
Check students' work

Page 53
Check students' work

Top of page 54
1. cousin; 2. pretty; 3. blue; 4. red; 5. two; 6. Leila

Bottom of page 54
1. c; 2. b; 3. d; 4. a

Top of page 59
1. T; 2. F; 3. T; 4. T; 5. F ; 6. T

Bottom of page 59
Check students' work

Top of page 60
Check students' work

Bottom of page 60
1. Peter is alone sitting at his desk.
2. Miles is spying on Peter.
3. Miles and Peter with Mr. Atkins and the mean older boys.

This Key Education product supports the NCTE/IRA Standards for the English Language Arts.

Each activity in *High-Interest/Low Readability: Miles Masters' Mystery Diaries* supports one or more of the following standards:

1. **Students read many different types of print and nonprint texts for a variety of purposes.**
Miles Masters' Mystery Diaries includes ten reading passages at varying reading levels, along with audio recordings of those passages to build both reading and listening skills.

2. **Students use a variety of strategies to build meaning while reading.**
Comprehension activities focusing on drawing conclusions, main idea, sequencing, inference, and vocabulary, among other skills, support this standard.

3. **Students communicate in spoken, written, and visual form, for a variety of purposes and a variety of audiences.**
Activities in *Miles Masters' Mystery Diaries* incorporate drawing and writing for a variety of purposes.

4. **Students use the writing process to write for different purposes and different audiences.**
Miles Masters' Mystery Diaries includes writing activities focused on a variety of audiences and purposes.

5. **Students incorporate knowledge of language conventions (grammar, spelling, punctuation), media techniques, and genre to create and discuss a variety of print and nonprint texts.**
Writing activities in *Miles Masters' Mystery Diaries* take different forms, from sentences to dialogues to advertisements, allowing students to practice different forms of writing and writing conventions.

6. **Students use spoken, written, and visual language for their own purposes, such as to learn, for enjoyment, or to share information.**
The engaging stories in *Miles Masters' Mystery Diaries* will motivate students to read independently and the skill-building activities will support students in becoming more effective independent readers and writers.